FAVORITE POEMS
for the GARDEN

A GARDENER'S COLLECTION

Copyright © 2022 by Bushel & Peck Books.

Published by Bushel & Peck Books, a family-run publishing house in Fresno, California, that believes in uplifting children with the highest standards of art, music, literature, and ideas. Find beautiful books for gifted young minds at www.bushelandpeckbooks.com.

Type set in Temeraire and Baskerville.
Watering can engraving by Bodor Tivadar/Shutterstock.com
Leaf engraving by MoreVector/Shutterstock.com

Designed by David Miles.

Bushel & Peck Books is dedicated to fighting illiteracy all over the world. For every book we sell, we donate one to a child in need—book for book. To nominate a school or organization to receive free books, please visit www.bushelandpeckbooks.com.

ISBN: 9781638191056

First Edition

Printed in the United States

10 9 8 7 6 5 4 3 2 1

FAVORITE
POEMS
for the GARDEN

A GARDENER'S COLLECTION

BUSHEL
& PECK
BOOKS

CONTENTS

EARTH

John Hall Wheelock

Grasshopper, your fairy song
And my poem alike belong
To the deep and silent earth
From which all poetry has birth;
All we say and all we sing
Is but as the murmuring
Of that drowsy heart of hers
When from her deep dream she stirs:
If we sorrow, or rejoice,
You and I are but her voice.

Deftly does the dust express
In mind her hidden loveliness,
And from her cool silence stream
The cricket's cry and Dante's dream:

For the earth that breeds the trees
Breeds cities too, and symphonies,
Equally her beauty flows
Into a savior or a rose.

Even as the growing grass
Up from the soil religions pass,
And the field that bears the rye
Bears parables and prophecy.
Out of the earth the poem grows
Like the lily, or the rose;
And all that man is or yet may be,
Is but herself in agony
Toiling up the steep ascent
Towards the complete accomplishment
When all dust shall be, the whole
Universe, one conscious soul.

Yea, and this my poem, too,
Is part of her as dust and dew,
Wherein herself she doth declare
Through my lips, and say her prayer.

PUTTING IN THE SEED

Robert Frost

You come to fetch me from my work to-night
When supper's on the table, and we'll see
If I can leave off burying the white
Soft petals fallen from the apple tree.

(Soft petals, yes, but not so barren quite,
Mingled with these, smooth bean and wrinkled pea;)
And go along with you ere you lose sight
Of what you came for and become like me,

Slave to a springtime passion for the earth.
How Love burns through the Putting in the Seed
On through the watching for that early birth
When, just as the soil tarnishes with weed,

The sturdy seedling with arched body comes
Shouldering its way and shedding the earth crumbs.

THE WHISPER OF THE EARTH

Edward J. O'Brien

In the misty hollow, shyly greening branches
Soften to the south wind, bending to the rain.
From the moistened earthland flutter little whispers,
Breathing hidden beauty, innocent of stain.

Little plucking fingers tremble through the grasses,
Little silent voices sigh the dawn of spring,
Little burning earth-flames break the awful stillness,
Little crying wind-sounds come before the King.

Powers, dominations urge the budding of the crocus,
Cherubim are singing in the moist cool stone,
Seraphim are calling through the channels of the lily,
God has heard the earth-cry and journeys to His throne.

IN A GARDEN

Horace Holley

I stood within a Garden during rain
Uncovering to the drops my lifted brow:
O joyous fancy, to imagine now
I slip, with trees and clouds, the social chain,
Alone with nature, naught to lose or gain
Nor even to become; no, just to be
A moment's personal essence, wholly free
From needs that mold the heart to forms of pain.
Arise, I cried, and celebrate the hour!
Acclaim serener gladness; if it fail,
New courage, nobler vision, will survive
That I have known my kinship to the flower,
My brotherhood with rain, and in this vale
Have been a moment's friend to all alive.

A SHOWER

Rowland Thirlmere

You may have seen, when winds were high,
That hesitant buds would not unfold
In garden-borders chill and dry,
Bright with the Easter-lilies' gold.
Then, suddenly, would come a shower—
The big breeze veering to the west—
And happier music filled the bower
Above the thrush's hidden nest:
The elm-tree's inconspicuous bloom
Vanished amidst her little leaves;
In box and bay a fragrant gloom
Inspired the wren's recitatives:
The woods assumed their delicate green
And spoke in songs that brought you bliss:
Ay, and your withered heart has been
Quickened on such a day as this!

THE RAIN

William H. Davies

———

I hear leaves drinking Rain;
    I hear rich leaves on top
Giving the poor beneath
    Drop after drop;
'Tis a sweet noise to hear
These green leaves drinking near.

And when the Sun comes out,
    After this Rain shall stop,
A wondrous Light will fill
    Each dark, round drop;
I hope the Sun shines bright;
'Twill be a lovely sight.

THE BIRTH OF THE FLOWERS

Mary McNeil Fenollosa

God spoke! and from the arid scene
Sprang rich and verdant bowers,
Till all the earth was soft with green,—
He smiled; and there were flowers.

TO A NEW SUNDIAL

Violet Fane

―――――――――

Oh, Sundial, you should not be young,
Or fresh and fair, or spick and span!
None should remember when began
Your tenure here, nor whence you sprung!

Like ancient cromlech notch'd and scarr'd,
I would have had you sadly tow'r
Above this world of leaf and flower
All ivy-tress'd and lichen-starr'd;

Ambassador of Time and Fate,
In contrast stern to bud and bloom,
Seeming half temple and half tomb,
And wholly solemn and sedate;

Till, one with God's own works on earth,
The lake, the vale, the mountain-brow,

We might have come to count you now
Whose home was here before our birth.

But lo! a priggish, upstart thing—
Set here to tell so old a truth—
How fleeting are our days of youth—
You, that were only made last spring!

Go to!... What sermon can you preach,
Oh, mushroom—mentor pert and new?
We are too old to learn of you
What you are all too young to teach!

Yet, Sundial, you and I may swear
Eternal friendship, none the less,
For I'll respect your youthfulness
If you'll forgive my silver hair!

THE FOUNTAIN

Harry Kemp

I thought my garden finished. I beheld
Each bush bee-visited; a green charm quelled
The louder winds to music; soft boughs made
Patches of silver dusk and purple shade—
And yet I felt a lack of something still.

There was a little, sleepy-footed rill
That lapsed among sun-burnished stones, where slept
Fish, rainbow-scaled, while dragon-flies, adept,
Balanced on bending grass.

       All perfect? No.
My garden lacked a fountain's upward flow.
I coaxed the brook's young Naiad to resign
Her meadow wildness, building her a shrine
Of worship, where each ravished waif of air
Might wanton in the brightness of her hair.

So here my fountain flows, loved of the wind,
To every vagrant, aimless gust inclined,
Yet constant ever to its source. It greets
The face of morning, wavering windy sheets
Of woven silver; sheer it climbs the noon,
A shaft of bronze; and underneath the moon
It sleeps in pearl and opal. In the storm
It streams far out, a wild, gray, blowing form;
While on calm days it heaps above the lake,—
Pelting the dreaming lilies half awake,
And pattering jewels on each wide, green frond,—
Recurrent pyramids of diamond!

THE WELCOME

Arthur Powell

God spreads a carpet soft and green
    O'er which we pass;
A thick-piled mat of jeweled sheen—
    And that is Grass.

Delightful music woos the ear;
    The grass is stirred
Down to the heart of every spear—
    Ah, that's a Bird.

Clouds roll before a blue immense
    That stretches high
And lends the soul exalted sense—
    That scroll's a Sky.

Green rollers flaunt their sparkling crests;
    Their jubilee

Extols brave Captains and their quests—
    And that is Sea.

New-leaping grass, the feathery flute,
    The sapphire ring,
The sea's full-voiced, profound salute,—
    Ah, this is Spring!

THE JOY OF THE SPRINGTIME

Sarojini Naidu

Springtime, O Springtime, what is your essence,
The lilt of a bulbul, the laugh of a rose,
The dance of the dew on the wings of a moonbeam,
The voice of the zephyr that sings as he goes,
The hope of a bride or the dream of a maiden
Watching the petals of gladness unclose?

Springtime, O Springtime, what is your secret,
The bliss at the core of your magical mirth,
That quickens the pulse of the morning to wonder
And hastens the seeds of all beauty to birth,
That captures the heavens and conquers to blossom
The roots of delight in the heart of the earth?

SPRING

John Gould Fletcher

At the first hour, it was as if one said, "Arise."
At the second hour, it was as if one said, "Go forth."
And the winter constellations that are like patient ox-eyes
Sank below the white horizon at the north.

At the third hour, it was as if one said, "I thirst;"
At the fourth hour, all the earth was still:
Then the clouds suddenly swung over, stooped, and burst;
And the rain flooded valley, plain and hill.

At the fifth hour, darkness took the throne;
At the sixth hour, the earth shook and the wind cried;
At the seventh hour, the hidden seed was sown,
At the eighth hour, it gave up the ghost and died.

At the ninth hour, they sealed up the tomb;
And the earth was then silent for the space of three hours.

But at the twelfth hour, a single lily from the gloom
Shot forth, and was followed by a whole host of flowers.

THE GREEN O' THE SPRING

Denis A. McCarthy

Sure, afther all the winther,
　An' afther all the snow,
'Tis fine to see the sunshine,
　'Tis fine to feel its glow;
'Tis fine to see the buds break
　On boughs that bare have been—
But best of all to Irish eyes
　'Tis grand to see the green!

Sure, afther all the winther,
　An' afther all the snow,
'Tis fine to hear the brooks sing
　As on their way they go;
'Tis fine to hear at mornin'
　The voice of robineen,
But best of all to Irish eyes
　'Tis grand to see the green!

Sure, here in grim New England
   The spring is always slow,
An' every bit o' green grass
   Is kilt wid frost and snow;
Ah, many a heart is weary
   The winther days, I ween
But oh, the joy when springtime comes
   An' brings the blessed green!

AN APRIL MORNING

Bliss Carman

Once more in misted April
The world is growing green.
Along the winding river
The plumey willows lean.

Beyond the sweeping meadows
The looming mountains rise,
Like battlements of dreamland
Against the brooding skies.

In every wooded valley
The buds are breaking through,
As though the heart of all things
No languor ever knew.

The golden-wings and bluebirds
Call to their heavenly choirs.

The pines are blued and drifted
With smoke of brushwood fires.

And in my sister's garden
Where little breezes run,
The golden daffodillies
Are blowing in the sun.

"PERHAPS YOU'D LIKE TO BUY A FLOWER?"

Emily Dickinson

Perhaps you'd like to buy a flower?
But I could never sell.
If you would like to borrow
Until the daffodil

Unties her yellow bonnet
Beneath the village door,
Until the bees, from clover rows
Their hock and sherry draw,

Why, I will lend until just then,
But not an hour more!

THE EARLY GODS

Witter Bynner

It is the time of violets.
    It is the very day
When in the shadow of the wood
    Spring shall have her say,
Remembering how the early gods
    Came up the violet way.
Are there not violets
    And gods—
    To-day?

THE CROCUS FLAME

Clinton Scollard

The Easter sunrise flung a bar of gold
O'er the awakening wold.
What was thine answer, O thou brooding earth,
What token of re-birth,
Of tender vernal mirth,
Thou the long-prisoned in the bonds of cold?

Under the kindling panoply which God
Spreads over tree and clod,
I looked far abroad.
Umber the sodden reaches seemed and seer
As when the dying year,
With rime-white sandals shod,
Faltered and fell upon its frozen bier.
Of some rathe quickening, some divine
Renascence not a sign!

And yet, and yet,

With touch of viol-chord, with mellow fret,

The lyric South amid the bough-tops stirred,

And one lone bird

An unexpected jet

Of song projected through the morning blue,

As though some wondrous hidden thing it knew.

And so I gathered heart, and cried again:

"O earth, make plain,

At this matutinal hour,

The triumph and the power

Of life eternal over death and pain,

Although it be but by some simple flower!"

And then, with sudden light,

Was dowered my veilèd sight,

And I beheld in a sequestered place

A slender crocus show its sun-bright face.

O miracle of Grace,

Earth's Easter answer came,

The revelation of transfiguring Might,

In that small crocus flame!

TULIPS

Arthur Guiterman

Brave little fellows in crimsons and yellows,
 Coming while breezes of April are cold,
Winter can't freeze you, he flies when he sees you
 Thrusting your spears through the redolent mold.

Jolly Dutch flowers, rejoicing in showers,
 Drink! ere the pageant of Spring passes by!
Hold your carousals to Robin's espousals,
 Lifting rich cups for the wine of the sky!

Dignified urbans in glossy silk turbans,
 Burgherlike blossoms of gardens and squares,
Nodding so solemn by fountain and column,
 What is the talk of your weighty affairs?

Pollen and honey (for such is your money),—
 Gossip and freight of the chaffering bee,—

Prospects of growing,—what colors are showing,—
  News of rare tulips from over the sea?

Loitering near you, how often I hear you,
  Just ere your petals at twilight are furled,
Laugh through the grasses while Evelyn passes,
  "There goes the loveliest flower in the world!"

A WHITE IRIS

Pauline B. Barrington

Tall and clothed in samite,
Chaste and pure,
In smooth armor,—
Your head held high
In its helmet
Of silver:
Jean D'Arc riding
Among the sword blades!

Has Spring for you
Wrought visions,
As it did for her
In a garden?

THE MAGNOLIA

José Santos Chocano

Deep in the wood, of scent and song the daughter,
Perfect and bright is the magnolia born;
White as a flake of foam upon still water,
White as soft fleece upon rough brambles torn.

Hers is a cup a workman might have fashioned
Of Grecian marble in an age remote.
Hers is a beauty perfect and impassioned,
As when a woman bares her rounded throat.

There is a tale of how the moon, her lover,
Holds her enchanted by some magic spell;
Something about a dove that broods above her,
Or dies within her breast—I cannot tell.

I cannot say where I have heard the story,
Upon what poet's lips; but this I know:
Her heart is like a pearl's, or like the glory
Of moonbeams frozen on the spotless snow.

MAY IS BUILDING HER HOUSE

Richard Le Gallienne

May is building her house. With apple blooms
She is roofing over the glimmering rooms;
Of the oak and the beech hath she builded its beams,
And, spinning all day at her secret looms,
With arras of leaves each wind-swayed wall
She pictureth over, and peopleth it all
    With echoes and dreams,
    And singing of streams.

May is building her house of petal and blade;
Of the roots of the oak is the flooring made,
    With a carpet of mosses and lichen and clover,
    Each small miracle over and over,
And tender, travelling green things strayed.

Her windows the morning and evening star,

And her rustling doorways, ever ajar
  With the coming and going
  Of fair things blowing,
The thresholds of the four winds are.

May is building her house. From the dust of things
She is making the songs and the flowers and the wings;
  From October's tossed and trodden gold
  She is making the young year out of the old;
  Yea! out of winter's flying sleet
  She is making all the summer sweet,
  And the brown leaves spurned of November's feet
She is changing back again to spring's.

JUNE RAPTURE

Angela Morgan

Green! What a world of green! My startled soul
Panting for beauty long denied,
Leaps in a passion of high gratitude
To meet the wild embraces of the wood;
Rushes and flings itself upon the whole
Mad miracle of green, with senses wide,
Clings to the glory, hugs and holds it fast,
As one who finds a long-lost love at last.
Billows of green that break upon the sight
In bounteous crescendos of delight,
Wind-hurried verdure hastening up the hills
To where the sun its highest rapture spills;
Cascades of color tumbling down the height
In golden gushes of delicious light—
God! Can I bear the beauty of this day,
Or shall I be swept utterly away?

Hush—here are deeps of green, where rapture stills,
Sheathing itself in veils of amber dusk;
Breathing a silence suffocating, sweet,
Wherein a million hidden pulses beat.
Look! How the very air takes fire and thrills
With hint of heaven pushing through her husk.
Ah, joy's not stopped! 'Tis only more intense,
Here where Creation's ardors all condense;
Here where I crush me to the radiant sod,
Close-folded to the very nerves of God.
See now—I hold my heart against this tree.
The life that thrills its trembling leaves thrills me.
There's not a pleasure pulsing through its veins
That does not sting me with ecstatic pains.
No twig or tracery, however fine,
Can bear a tale of joy exceeding mine.

Praised be the gods that made my spirit mad;
Kept me aflame and raw to beauty's touch.
Lashed me and scourged me with the whip of fate;
Gave me so often agony for mate;
Tore from my heart the things that make men glad—
Praised be the gods! If I at last, by such
Relentless means may know the sacred bliss,
The anguished rapture of an hour like this.

Smite me, O Life, and bruise me if thou must;
Mock me and starve me with thy bitter crust,
But keep me thus aquiver and awake,
Enamoured of my life for living's sake!
This were the tragedy—that I should pass,
Dull and indifferent through the glowing grass.
And this the reason I was born, I say—
That I might know the passion of this day!

COLUMBINES

Arthur Guiterman

Late were we sleeping
Deep in the mold,
Clasping and keeping
Yesterday's gold—
Hoardings of sunshine,
Crimson and gold;
Dreaming of light till our dream became
Aureate bells and beakers of flame,—
Splashed with the splendor of wine of flame.
Raindrop awoke us;
Zephyr bespoke us;
Chick-a-dee called us,
Bobolink called us,—
Then we came.

THE MORNING-GLORY

Florence Earle Coates

Was it worth while to paint so fair
    Thy every leaf—to vein with faultless art
Each petal, taking the boon light and air
    Of summer so to heart?

To bring thy beauty unto perfect flower,
    Then, like a passing fragrance or a smile,
Vanish away, beyond recovery's power—
    Was it, frail bloom, worth while?

Thy silence answers: "Life was mine!
    And I, who pass without regret or grief,
Have cared the more to make my moment fine,
    Because it was so brief.

"In its first radiance I have seen
    The sun!—why tarry then till comes the night?
I go my way, content that I have been
    Part of the morning light!"

LARKSPUR

James Oppenheim

Blue morning and the beloved,
The hill-garden and I ...

Blue morning and the beloved,
Leaning, laughing and plucking,
Plucking wet roses ...

    (She among the roses,
    I among the larkspur,
    Bob-white, warbler, meadowlark, bobolink,
    Song, sun,
    And still morning air.)

I snipped off a larkspur blossom of china-blue
And held it,
A blossom against the sky ...

And heaven opened out
In one small flower-face ...

And the beloved,
Plucking roses, plucking roses, old-fashioned roses,
Lifted her face
With eyes of china-blue.

(She among the roses,
I among the larkspur,
Bee-hum, brown-mole, downy chick, humming-bird:
Light, dew,
And laughter of my love.)

THE JULY GARDEN

Robert Ernest Vernède

It's July in my garden; and steel-blue are the globe thistles
And French grey the willows that bow to every breeze;
And deep in every currant bush a robber blackbird
    whistles
"I'm picking, I'm picking, I'm picking these!"
So off I go to rout them, and find instead I'm gazing
At clusters of delphiniums—the seed was small and
    brown,
But these are spurs that fell from heaven and caught the
    most amazing
Colours of the welkin's own as they came hustling down.
And then some roses catch my eye, or may be some Sweet
    Williams
Or pink and white and purple peals of Canterbury bells
Or pencilled Violas that peep between the three-leaved
    trilliums

Or red-hot pokers all aglow or poppies that cast spells—
And while I stare at each in turn I quite forget or pardon
The blackbirds—and the blackguards—that keep robbing
　　me of pie;
For what do such things matter when I have so fair a
　　garden
And what is half so lovely as my garden in July?

MID-SUMMER BLOOMS

Emile Verhaeren

Mid-summer blooms within our quiet garden-ways;
A golden peacock down the dusky alley strays;
    Gay flower petals strew
        —Pearl, emerald and blue—
The curving slopes of fragrant summer grass;
    The pools are clear as glass
Between the white cups of the lily-flowers;
The currants are like jewelled fairy-bowers;
A dazzling insect worries the heart of a rose,
Where a delicate fern a filmy shadow throws,
And airy as bubbles the thousands of bees
Over the young grape-clusters swarm as they please.

The air is pearly, iridescent, pure;
These profound and radiant noons mature,
Unfolding even as odorous roses of clear light;

Familiar roads to distances invite
Like slow and graceful gestures, one by one
Bound for the pearly-hued horizon and the sun.

Surely the summer clothes, with all her arts,
No other garden with such grace and power;
And 'tis the poignant joy close-folded in our hearts
That cries its life aloud from every flaming flower.

POPPIES

John Russell Hayes

O perfect flowers of sweet midsummer days,
 The season's emblems ye,
 As nodding lazily
Ye kiss to sleep each breeze that near you strays,
 And soothe the tired gazer's sense
With lulling surges of your softest somnolence.

Like fairy lamps ye light the garden bed
 With tender ruby glow.
 Not any flowers that blow
Can match the glory of your gleaming red;
 Such sunny-warm and dreamy hue
Before ye lit your fires no garden ever knew.

Bright are the blossoms of the scarlet sage,
 And bright the velvet vest

On the nasturtium's breast;
Bright are the tulips when they reddest rage,
    And bright the coreopsis' eye;—
But none of all can with your brilliant beauty vie.

O soft and slumberous flowers, we love you well;
    Your glorious crimson tide
    The mossy walk beside
Holds all the garden in its drowsy spell;
    And walking there we gladly bless
Your queenly grace and all your languorous loveliness.

THE GARDEN IN AUGUST

Gertrude Huntington McGiffert

From corn-crib by the level pasture-lands
To knoll where spruce and boulders hide the road
I know it like a book, and when my heart
Is waste and dry and hard and choked with weeds,
I come here till it gently blooms again.
For gardens yield rich fruits that will outlast
The autumn and the winter of the soul,
Richest to him who toils with loving hands.
'Tis delving thus we learn life's secrets told
But to those favored few who dig for them.
The Garden is an intimate and keeps
In touch with us, yet hath its own high moods,
And doth impose them on the mind of man
To shame his pettiness. So do I love
Its shimmering August mood keyed to the sun,
A harlequin of color, birds and bloom.

Nasturtiums, zinnias, balsams, salvias blaze
By vivid dahlias; tiger-lilies burn
In scarlet shadow of Jerusalem-cross;
Beyond the queen-hydrangeas splendid rule
Barbaric marigolds; chrysanthemums
Outshine gladioli, and sunflowers flaunt
Their crests of gold beneath the giant gourds.
Within the arbor, script forgot, I muse,
While gorgeous hollyhocks sway to and fro
To mark the silences, and butterflies
Flit in and out like some bright memory,
And blinding poppies kindle slow watch-fires
Before the golden altar of the sun.

A spell lies on the Garden. Summer sits
With finger on her lips as if she heard
The steps of Autumn echo on the hill.
A hush lies on the Garden. Summer dreams
Of timid crocus thrust through drifted snow.

SUNFLOWERS

Clinton Scollard

My tall sunflowers love the sun,
　　Love the burning August noons
When the locust tunes its viol,
　　And the cricket croons.

When the purple night draws on,
　　With its planets hung on high,
And the attared winds of slumber
　　Wander down the sky,

Still my sunflowers love the sun,
　　Keep their ward and watch and wait
Till the rosy key of morning
　　Opes the eastern gate.

Then, when they have deeply quaffed
　　From the brimming cups of dew,
You can hear their golden laughter
　　All the garden through.

THE END OF SUMMER

Edna St. Vincent Millay

When poppies in the garden bleed,
And coreopsis goes to seed,
And pansies, blossoming past their prime,
Grow small and smaller all the time,
When on the mown field, shrunk and dry,
Brown dock and purple thistle lie,
And smoke from forest fires at noon
Can make the sun appear the moon,
When apple seeds, all white before,
Begin to darken in the core,
I know that summer, scarcely here,
Is gone until another year.

THE SNOW-GARDENS

Zoë Akins

———

Like an empty stage
The gardens are empty and cold;
The marble terraces rise
Like vases that hold no flowers;
The lake is frozen, the fountain still;
The marble walls and the seats
Are useless and beautiful.
Ah, here
Where the wind and the dusk and the snow are
All is silent and white and sad!
Why do I think of you?
Why does your name remorselessly
Strike through my heart?
Why does my soul awaken and shudder?
Why do I seem to hear
Cries as lovely as music?
Surely you never came

Into these pale snow-gardens;

Surely you never stood

Here in the twilight with me;

Yet here I have lingered and dreamed

Of a face as subtle as music,

Of golden hair, and of eyes

Like a child's ...

I have felt on my brow

Your finger-tips, plaintive as music ...

O Wonder of all wonders, O Love—

Wrought of sweet sounds and of dreaming!—

Why do you not emerge

From the lilac pale petals of dusk,

And come to me here in the gardens

Where the wind and the snow are?

Beauty and Peace are here—

And unceasing music—

And a loneliness chill and wistful,

Like the feeling of death.

Like a crystal lily a star

Leans from its leaves of silver

And gleams in the sky;

And golden and faint in the shadows

You wait indistinctly,—

Like a phantom lamp that appears
In the mirror of distance that hovers
By the window at twilight—
You have come—and we stand together,
With questioning eyes—
Dreaming and cold and ghostly
In an empty garden that seems
Like an empty stage.

THE GARDEN

Gertrude Huntington McGiffert

Old gardens have a language of their own,
And mine sweet speech to linger in the heart.
A goodly place it is and primly spaced,
With straight box-bordered paths and squares of bloom.
Bay-trees by rows of antique urns tell tales
Of one who loved the gardens Dante loved.
Magnolias edge the placid lily-pool
And flank the sagging seat, whence vista leads
To blaze of rhododendrons banked in green.
Azaleas by the scarlet quince flame up
Against the lustrous grape-vines trellised high
To pigeon-cote and old brick wall where hide
First snowdrops and the bravest violets.
A place of solitudes whose silences
Enfold the heart as an unquiet bird.

THE OLD-FASHIONED GARDEN

John Russell Hayes

Among the meadows of the countryside,
    From city noise and tumult far away,
Where clover-blossoms spread their fragrance wide
    And birds are warbling all the sunny day,
There is a spot which lovingly I prize,
For there a fair and sweet old-fashioned country garden lies.

The gray old mansion down beside the lane
    Stands knee-deep in the fields that lie around
And scent the air with hay and ripening grain.
    Behind the manse box-hedges mark the bound
And close the garden in, or nearly close,
For on beyond the hollyhocks an olden orchard grows.

So bright and lovely is the dear old place,
    It seems as though the country's very heart
Were centered here, and that its antique grace

Must ever hold it from the world apart.
Immured it lies among the meadows deep,
Its flowery stillness beautiful and calm as softest sleep.

The morning-glories ripple o'er the hedge
    And fleck its greenness with their tinted foam;
Sweet wilding things, up to the garden's edge
    They love to wander from their meadow home,
To take what little pleasure here they may
Ere all their silken trumpets close before the warm midday.

The larkspur lifts on high its azure spires,
    And up the arbor's lattices are rolled
The quaint nasturtium's many-colored fires;
    The tall carnation's breast of faded gold
Is striped with many a faintly-flushing streak,
Pale as the tender tints that blush upon a baby's cheek.

The old sweet-rocket sheds its fine perfumes,
    With golden stars the coreopsis flames,
And here are scores of sweet old-fashioned blooms,
    Dear for the very fragrance of their names,—
Poppies and gilly flowers and four-o'clocks,
Cowslips and candytuft and heliotrope and hollyhocks,

Harebells and peonies and dragon-head,
    Petunias, scarlet sage and bergamot,
Verbenas, ragged-robins, soft gold-thread,
    The bright primrose and pale forget-me-not,
Wall-flowers and crocuses and columbines,
Narcissus, asters, hyacinths, and honeysuckle vines.

A sweet seclusion this of sun and shade,
    A calm asylum from the busy world,
Where greed and restless care do ne'er invade,
    Nor news of 'change and mart each morning hurled
Round half the globe; no noise of party feud
Disturbs this peaceful spot nor mars its perfect quietude.

But summer after summer comes and goes
    And leaves the garden ever fresh and fair;
May brings the tulip, golden June the rose,
    And August winds shake down the mellow pear.
Man blooms and blossoms, fades and disappears,—
But scarce a tribute pays the garden to the passing years.

Sweet is the odor of the warm, soft rain
    In violet-days when spring opes her green heart;
And sweet the apple trees along the lane
    Whose lovely blossoms all too soon depart;

And sweet the brimming dew that overfills

The golden chalices of all the trembling daffodils.

But sweeter far, in this old garden-close

    To loiter 'mid the lovely old-time flowers,

To breathe the scent of lavender and rose,

    And with old poets pass the peaceful hours.

Old gardens and old poets,—happy he

Whose quiet summer days are spent in such sweet company!

IN MY MOTHER'S GARDEN

Margaret Widdemer

There were many flowers in my mother's garden,
Sword-leaved gladiolas, taller far than I,
Sticky-leaved petunias, pink and purple flaring,
Velvet-painted pansies smiling at the sky;

Scentless portulacas crowded down the borders,
White and scarlet-petalled, rose and satin-gold,
Clustered sweet alyssum, lacy-white and scented,
Sprays of gray-green lavender to keep 'til you were old.

In my mother's garden were green-leaved hiding-places,
Nooks between the lilacs—oh, a pleasant place to play!
Still my heart can hide there, still my eyes can dream it,
Though the long years lie between and I am far away;

When the world is hard now, when the city's clanging
Tires my eyes and tires my heart and dust lies everywhere,

I can dream the peace still of the soft wind's blowing,
I can be a child still and hide my heart from care.

Lord, if still that garden blossoms in the sunlight,
Grant that children laugh there now among its green and
    gold—
Grant that little hearts still hide its memoried sweetness,
Locking one bright dream away for light when they are old!

ASKING FOR ROSES

Robert Frost

A house that lacks, seemingly, mistress and master,
    With doors that none but the wind ever closes,
Its floor all littered with glass and with plaster;
    It stands in a garden of old-fashioned roses.

I pass by that way in the gloaming with Mary;
    "I wonder," I say, "who the owner of those is."
"Oh, no one you know," she answers me airy,
    "But one we must ask if we want any roses."

So we must join hands in the dew coming coldly
    There in the hush of the wood that reposes,
And turn and go up to the open door boldly,
    And knock to the echoes as beggars for roses.

"Pray, are you within there, Mistress Who-were-you?"
    'Tis Mary that speaks and our errand discloses.

"Pray are you within there? Bestir you, bestir you!
    'Tis summer again; there's two come for roses.

"A word with you, that of the singer recalling—
    Old Herrick: a saying that every man knows is
A flower unplucked is but left to the falling,
    And nothing is gained by not gathering roses."

We do not loosen our hands' intertwining
    (Not caring so very much what she supposes),
There when she comes on us mistily shining
    And grants us by silence the boon of her roses.

STAIRWAYS AND GARDENS

Ella Wheeler Wilcox

Gardens and Stairways; those are words that thrill me
Always with vague suggestions of delight.
Stairways and Gardens. Mystery and grace
Seem part of their environment; they fill all space
With memories of things veiled from my sight
In some far place.

Gardens. The word is overcharged with meaning;
It speaks of moonlight, and a closing door;
Of birds at dawn—of sultry afternoons.
Gardens. I seem to see low branches screening
A vine-roofed arbor with a leaf-tiled floor
Where sunlight swoons.

Stairways. The word winds upward to a landing,
Then curves and vanishes in space above.
Lights fall, lights rise; soft lights that meet and blend.

Stairways; and some one at the bottom standing
Expectantly with lifted looks of love.
Then steps descend.

Gardens and Stairways. They belong with song—
With subtle scents of perfume, myrrh and musk—
With dawn and dusk—with youth, romance, and mystery,
And times that were and times that are to be.
Stairways and Gardens.

TO A WEED

Gertrude Hall

You bold thing! thrusting 'neath the very nose
Of her fastidious majesty, the rose,
Even in the best ordainèd garden bed,
Unauthorized, your smiling little head!

The gardener, mind! will come in his big boots,
And drag you up by your rebellious roots,
And cast you forth to shrivel in the sun,
Your daring quelled, your little weed's life done.

And when the noon cools, and the sun drops low,
He'll come again with his big wheelbarrow,
And trundle you—I don't know clearly where,
But off, outside the dew, the light, the air.

Meantime—ah, yes! the air is very blue,
And gold the light, and diamond the dew,—

You laugh and courtesy in your worthless way,
And you are gay, ah, so exceeding gay!

You argue in your manner of a weed,
You did not make yourself grow from a seed,
You fancy you've a claim to standing-room,
You dream yourself a right to breathe and bloom.

The sun loves you, you think, just as the rose,
He never scorned you for a weed,—he knows!
The green-gold flies rest on you and are glad,
It's only cross old gardeners find you bad.

You know, you weed, I quite agree with you,
I am a weed myself, and I laugh too,—
Both, just as long as we can shun his eye,
Let's sniff at the old gardener trudging by!

THE THISTLE

Miles M. Dawson

Ha, prickle-armèd knight,
　　How oft the world hath cursed thee,
Thou pestilence of Earth,
　　The beldame who hath nursed thee!

Hath hellish Proserpine
　　Her needs lent to arm thee
That mischief-loving gods,
　　Pricked sorely, may not harm thee?

Or hath the mirthful Love
　　Presented thee his pinions
To dress thy tiny seeds,
　　The curse of man's dominions!

Thou like a maiden art
　　Who best can find protection

Employed at needlework
    From idleness' infection.

And like a prude thou art
    When he who loves embraces;
Thou dost repel with thorns
    And she with sharper phrases.

And like the wraith thou art
    Wherewith my heart is haunted;
Ye both take most delight
    Where ye the least are wanted.

WILD GARDENS

Ada Foster Murray

On the ripened grass is a bloomy mist
Of silver and rose and amethyst
　　Where the long June wave has run.

There are glints of copper and tarnished brass,
And hyacinthine flames that pass
　　From the green fires of the sun.

This web of a thousand gleams and glows
Was woven silently out of the snows
　　And the patient shine and rain.

It was fashioned cunningly day by day
From the silken spear to the pollened spray
　　With its folded sheaths of grain.

Oh, garden of grasses deep and wild,
So dear to the vagrant and the child
    And the singer of an hour.

To the wayworn soul you give your balm,
Your cup of peace, your stringèd psalm,
    Your grace of bud and flower.

A SOFT DAY

W. M. Letts

A soft day, thank God!
A wind from the south
With a honeyed mouth;
A scent of drenching leaves,
Briar and beech and lime,
White elder-flower and thyme
And the soaking grass smells sweet,
Crushed by my two bare feet,
While the rain drips,
Drips, drips, drips from the eaves.

A soft day, thank God!
The hills wear a shroud
Of silver cloud;
The web the spider weaves

Is a glittering net;
The woodland path is wet,
And the soaking earth smells sweet
Under my two bare feet,
And the rain drips,
Drips, drips, drips from the eaves.

BUT WE DID WALK IN EDEN

Josephine Preston Peabody

But we did walk in Eden,
    Eden, the garden of God;—
There, where no beckoning wonder
Of all the paths we trod,
No choiring sun-filled vineyard,
No voice of stream or bird,
But was some radiant oracle
And flaming with the Word!

Mine ears are dim with voices;
Mine eyes yet strive to see
The black things here to wonder at,
The mirth,—the misery.
Beloved, who wert with me there,
    How came these shames to be?—
    On what lost star are we?

Men say: The paths of gladness
    By men were never trod!—
But we have walked in Eden,
    Eden, the garden of God.

HEART'S GARDEN

Norreys Jephson O'Conor

I have a garden filled with many flowers:
The mignonette, the sweet-pea, and the rose,
Daisies, and daffodils, whose color glows
The fairer for the verdure which embowers
Their beauty, and sets forth their hidden powers
To charm my heart, whenever at the close
Of day's dull hurry I would seek repose
In my still garden through the darkening hours.

Thus, Lady, do I keep a place apart,
Wherein my love for you cloistered shall be,
Far from the rattle of the city cart,
Even as my garden, where daily I may see
The flowers of your love, and none from me
May win the hidden secret of my heart.

A ROSE LOVER

Frederic A. Whiting

Do thou, my rose, incline
Thy heart to mine.
If love be real
Ah, whisper, whisper low
That I at last may know.
Quick! breathe it now!
A sigh,—a tear,—a vow:
Oh, any lightest thing
Its cadences to sing
That loved am I, and not,
Ah, not forgot!

THE AWAKENING

Angela Morgan

You little, eager, peeping thing—
You embryonic point of light
Pushing from out your winter night,
How you do make my pulses sing!
A tiny eye amid the gloom—
The merest speck I scarce had seen—
So doth God's rapture rend the tomb
In this wee burst of April green!

And lo, 'tis here—and lo! 'Tis there—
Spurting its jets of sweet desire
In upward curling threads of fire
Like tapers kindling all the air.
Why, scarce it seems an hour ago
These branches clashed in bitter cold;
What Power hath set their veins aglow?

O soul of mine, be bold, be bold!
If from this tree, this blackened thing,
Hard as the floor my feet have prest,
This flame of joy comes clamoring
In hues as red as robin's breast
Waking to life this little twig—
O faith of mine, be big! Be big!

SHADE

Theodosia Garrison

The kindliest thing God ever made,
His hand of very healing laid
Upon a fevered world, is shade.

His glorious company of trees
Throw out their mantles, and on these
The dust-stained wanderer finds ease.

Green temples, closed against the beat
Of noontime's blinding glare and heat,
Open to any pilgrim's feet.

The white road blisters in the sun;
Now, half the weary journey done,
Enter and rest, Oh, weary one!

And feel the dew of dawn still wet
Beneath thy feet, and so forget
The burning highway's ache and fret.

This is God's hospitality,
And whoso rests beneath a tree
Hath cause to thank Him gratefully.

THE TREE

Evelyn Underhill

Spread, delicate roots of my tree,

Feeling, clasping, thrusting, growing;

Sensitive pilgrim root tips roaming everywhere.

Into resistant earth your filaments forcing,

Down in the dark, unknown, desirous:

The strange ceaseless life of you, eating and drinking of
earth,

The corrosive secretions of you, breaking the stuff of the
world to your will.

Tips of my tree in the springtime bursting to terrible beauty,

Folded green life, exquisite, holy exultant;

I feel in you the splendour, the autumn of ripe fulfilment,

Love and labour and death, the sacred pageant of life.

In the sweet curled buds of you,

In the opening glory of leaves, tissues moulded of green
light;

Veined, cut, perfect to type,
Each one like a child of high lineage bearing the sigil of
  race.

The open hands of my tree held out to the touch of the air
As love that opens its arms and waits on the lover's will;
The curtsey, the sway, and the toss of the spray as it sports
  with the breeze;
Rhythmical whisper of leaves that murmur and move in the
  light;
Crying of wind in the boughs, the beautiful music of pain:
Thus do you sing and say
The sorrow, the effort, the sweet surrender, the joy.

Come! tented leaves of my tree;
High summer is here, the moment of passionate life,
The hushed, the maternal hour.
Deep in the shaded green your mystery shielding,
Heir of the ancient woods and parent of forests to be,
Lo! to your keeping is given the Father's life-giving thought;
The thing that is dream and deed and carries the gift of the
  past.
For this, for this, great tree,
The glory of maiden leaves, the solemn stretch of the bough,
The wise persistent roots

Into the stuff of the world their filaments forcing,
Breaking the earth to their need.

Tall tree, your name is peace.
You are the channel of God:
His mystical sap,
Elixir of infinite love, syrup of infinite power,
Swelling and shaping, brooding and hiding,
With out-thrust of delicate joy, with pitiless pageant of
    death,
Sings in your cells;
Its rhythmical cycle of life
In you is fulfilled.

LOVELIEST OF TREES

A. E. Housman

Loveliest of trees, the cherry now
Is hung with bloom along the bough,
And stands about the woodland ride
Wearing white for Eastertide.

Now, of my threescore years and ten,
Twenty will not come again,
And take from seventy springs a score,
It only leaves me fifty more.

And since to look at things in bloom
Fifty springs are little room,
About the woodlands I will go
To see the cherry hung with snow.

IN AN OLD GARDEN

Madison Cawein

Old phantoms haunt it of the long-ago;
Old ghosts of old-time lovers and of dreams:
Within the quiet sunlight there, meseems,
I see them walking where those lilies blow.
The hardy phlox sways to some garments' flow;
The salvia there with sudden scarlet streams,
Caught from some ribbon of some throat that gleams,
Petunia fair, in flounce and furbelow.
I seem to hear their whispers in each wind
That wanders 'mid the flowers. There they stand!
Among the shadows of that apple tree!
They are not dead, whom still it keeps in mind,
This garden, planted by some lovely hand
That keeps it fragrant with its memory.

THE GARDEN OF DREAMS

Bliss Carman

My heart is a garden of dreams
Where you walk when day is done,
Fair as the royal flowers,
Calm as the lingering sun.

Never a drouth comes there,
Nor any frost that mars,
Only the wind of love
Under the early stars,—

The living breath that moves
Whispering to and fro,
Like the voice of God in the dusk
Of the garden long ago.

HOMESICK

Julia C. R. Dorr

O my garden! lying whitely in the moonlight and the dew,
Far across the leagues of distance flies my heart to-night to you,
And I see your stately lilies in the tender radiance gleam
With a dim, mysterious splendor, like the angels of a dream!

I can see the stealthy shadows creep along the ivied wall,
And the bosky depths of verdure where the drooping vine-
    leaves fall,
And the tall trees standing darkly with their crowns against
    the sky,
While overhead the harvest moon goes slowly sailing by.

I can see the trellised arbor, and the roses' crimson glow,
And the lances of the larkspurs all glittering, row on row,
And the wilderness of hollyhocks, where brown bees seek their
    spoil,
And butterflies dance all day long, in glad and gay turmoil.

O, the broad paths running straightly, north and south and
   east and west!
O, the wild grape climbing sturdily to reach the oriole's nest!
O, the bank where wild flowers blossom, ferns nod and mosses
   creep
In a tangled maze of beauty over all the wooded steep!

Just beyond the moonlit garden I can see the orchard trees,
With their dark boughs overladen, stirring softly in the breeze,
And the shadows on the greensward, and within the pasture
   bars
The white sheep huddling quietly beneath the pallid stars.

O my garden! lying whitely in the moonlight and the dew,
Far across the restless ocean flies my yearning heart to you,
And I turn from storied castle, hoary fane, and ruined shrine,
To the dear, familiar pleasaunce where my own white lilies
   shine—

With a vague, half-startled wonder if some night in Paradise,
From the battlements of heaven I shall turn my longing eyes
All the dim, resplendent spaces and the mazy stardrifts
   through
To my garden lying whitely in the moonlight and the dew!

ABOUT BUSHEL & PECK BOOKS

Bushel & Peck Books is a children's publishing house with a special mission. Through our Book-for-Book Promise™, we donate one book to kids in need for every book we sell. Our beautiful books are given to kids through schools, libraries, local neighborhoods, shelters, nonprofits, and also to many selfless organizations that are working hard to make a difference. So thank you for purchasing this book! Because of you, another book will make its way into the hands of a child who needs it most.

NOMINATE A SCHOOL OR ORGANIZATION TO RECEIVE FREE BOOKS

Do you know a school, library, or organization that could use some free books for their kids? We'd love to help! Please fill out the nomination form on our website (see below), and we'll do everything we can to make something happen.

www.bushelandpeckbooks.com/pages/
nominate-a-school-or-organization

If you liked this book, please leave a review online at your favorite retailer. Honest reviews spread the word about Bushel & Peck—and help us make better books, too!

Printed in the United States
by Baker & Taylor Publisher Services